MODERN
HOUSES

MW00890323

MINIMALIST ART
COLORING BOOK
50 DESIGNS

ISBN: 9798867048617
Publisher: Independently Published

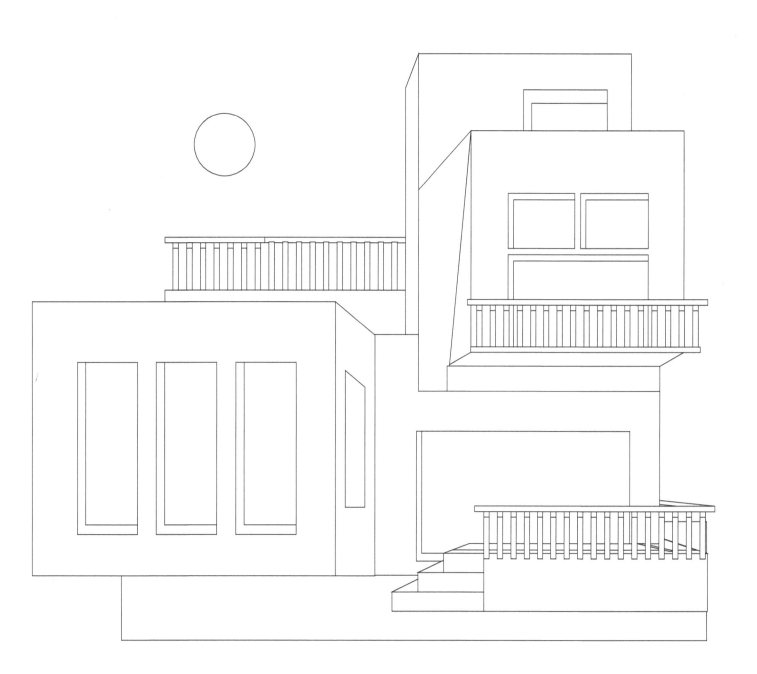

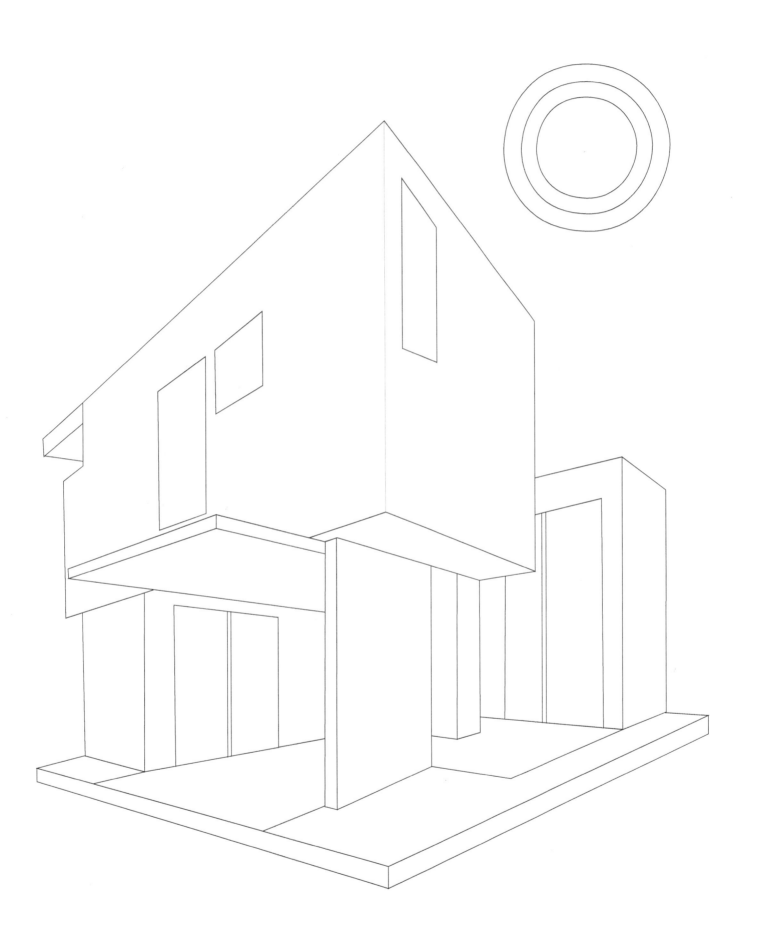

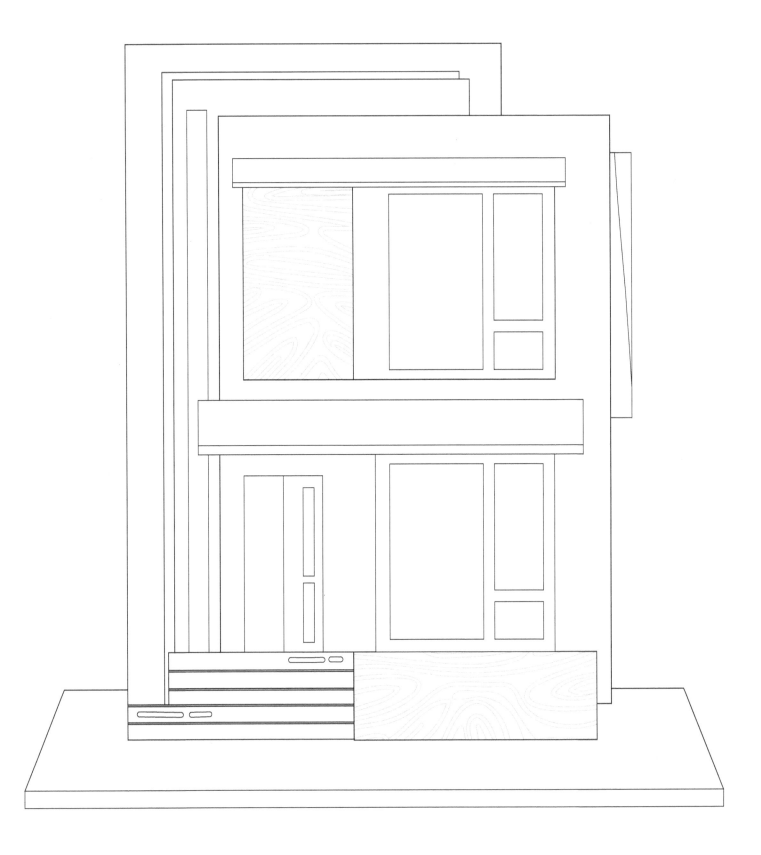

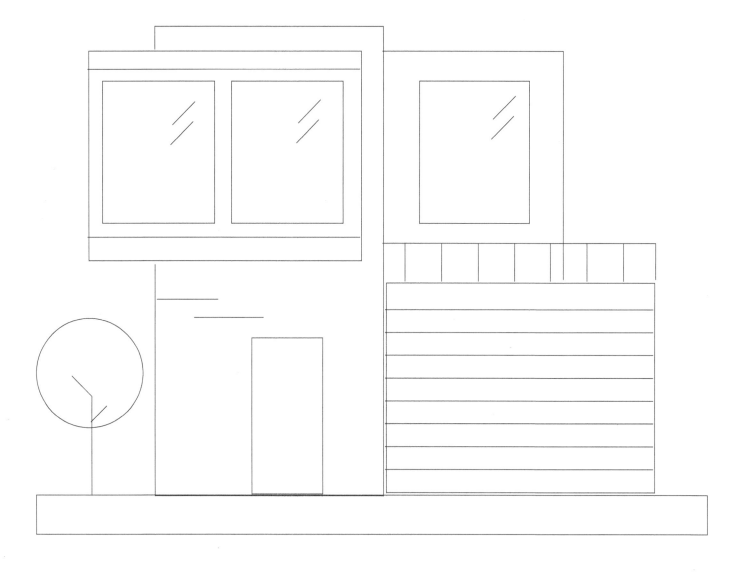

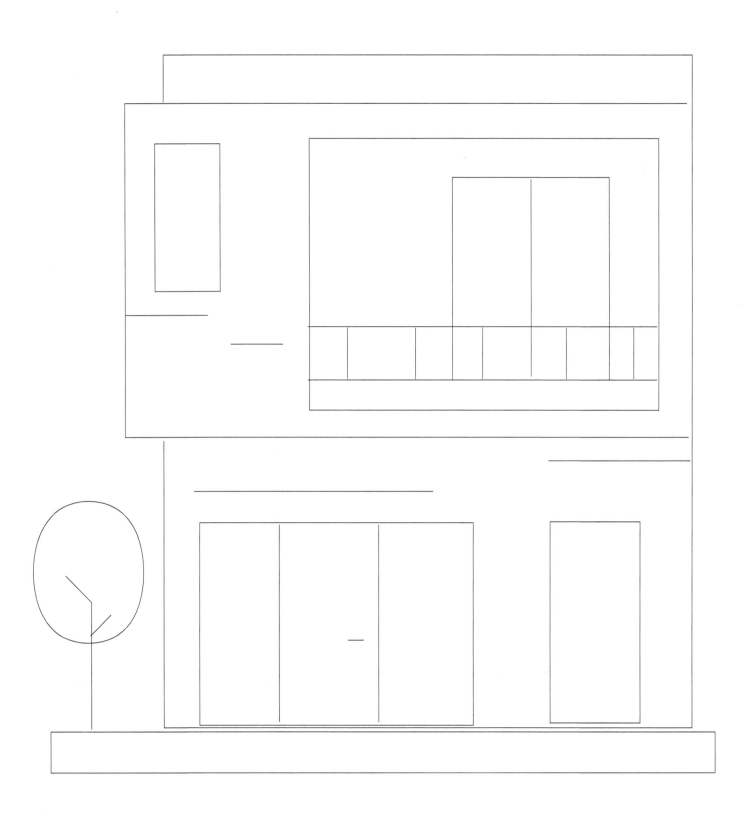

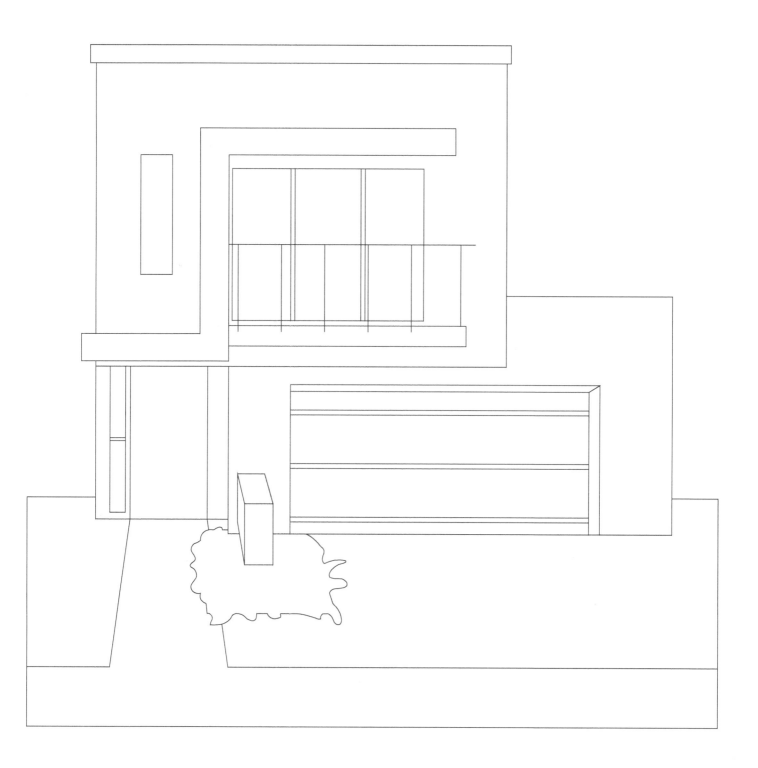

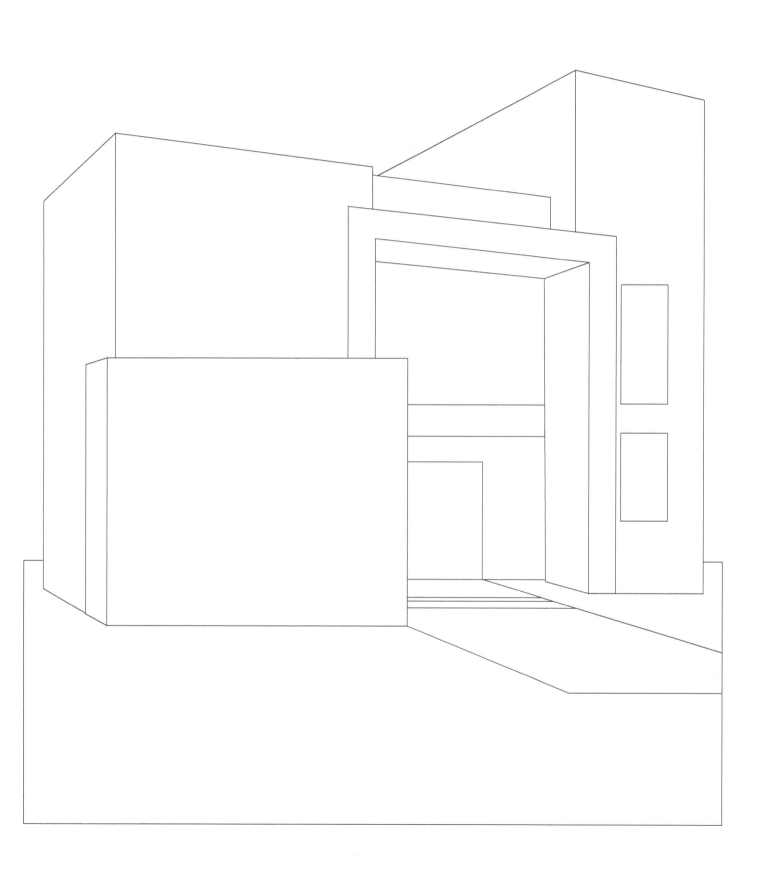

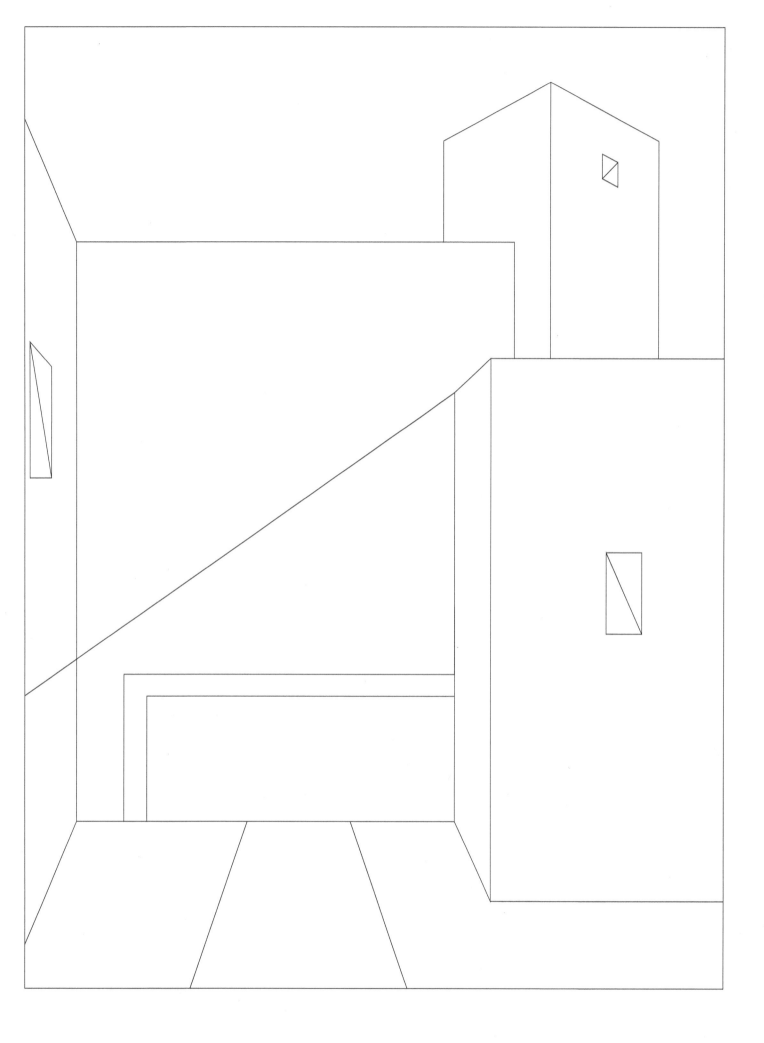

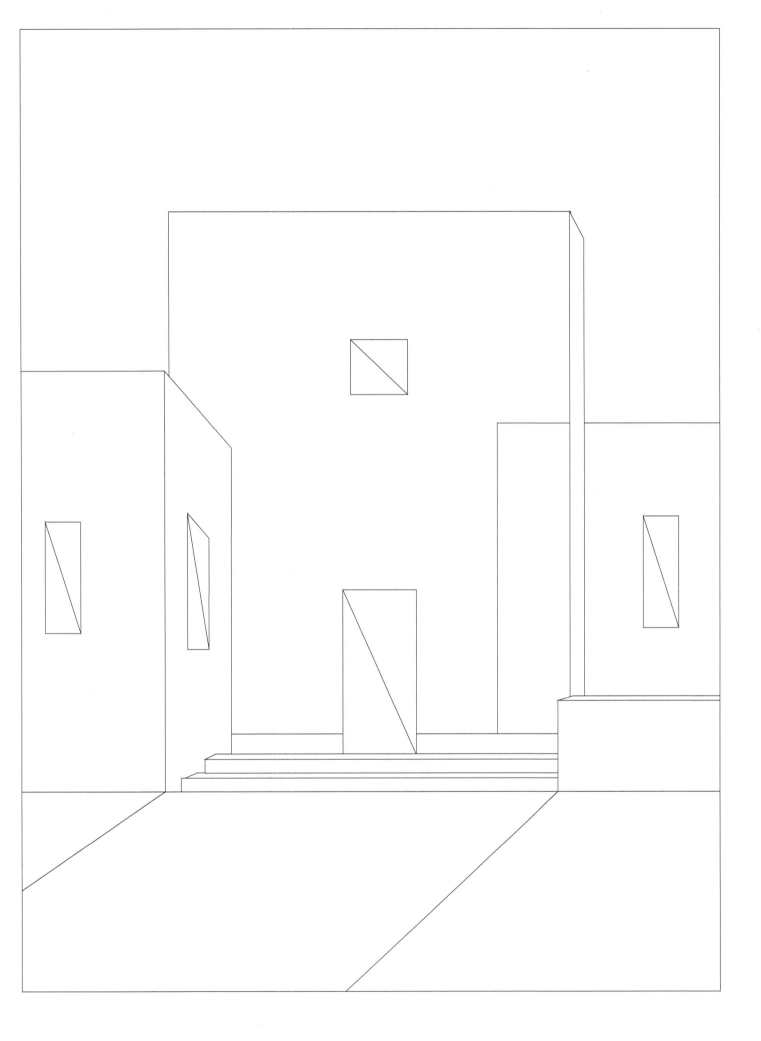

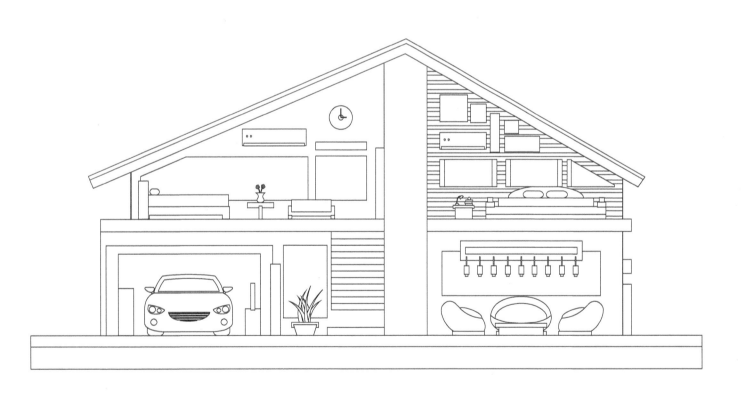

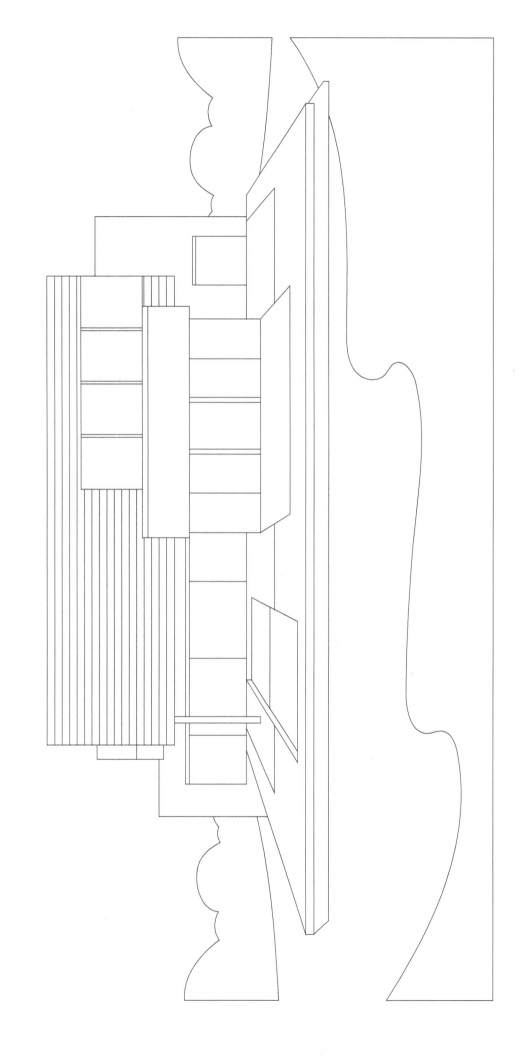

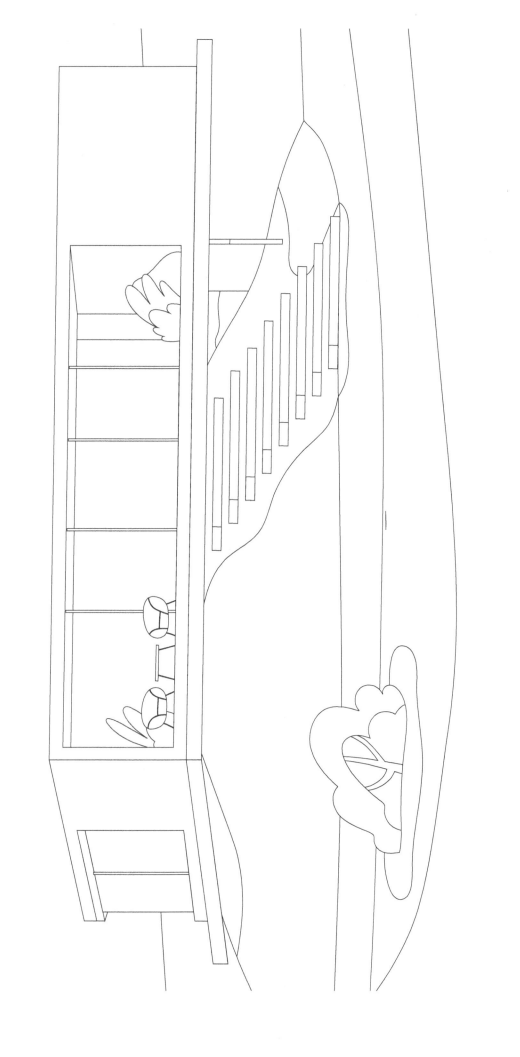

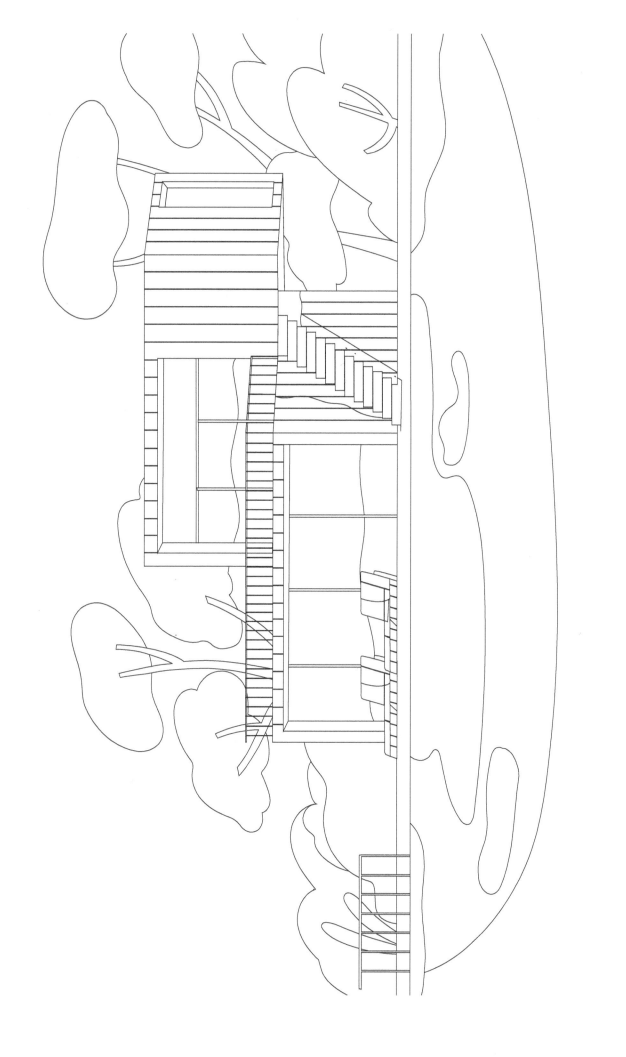

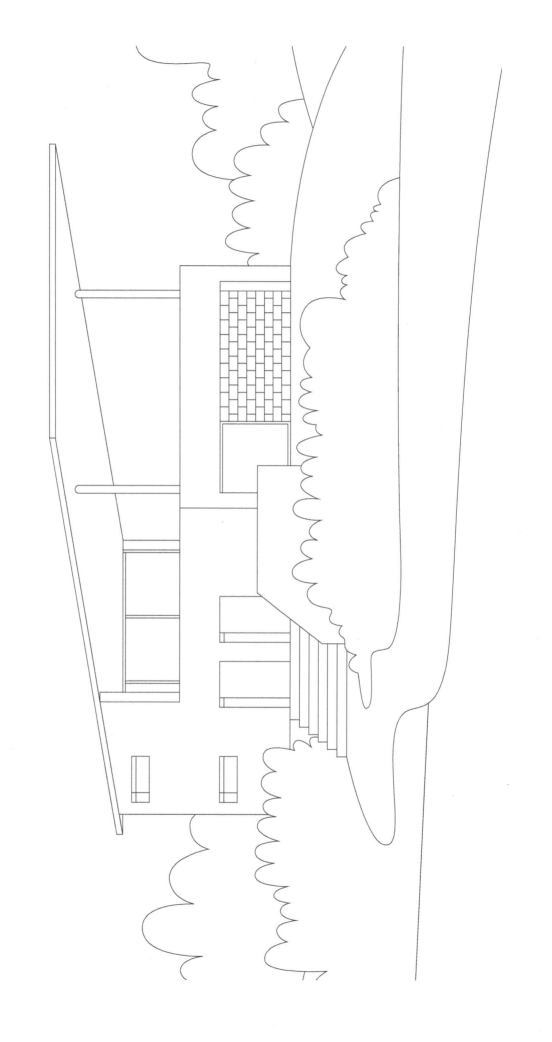

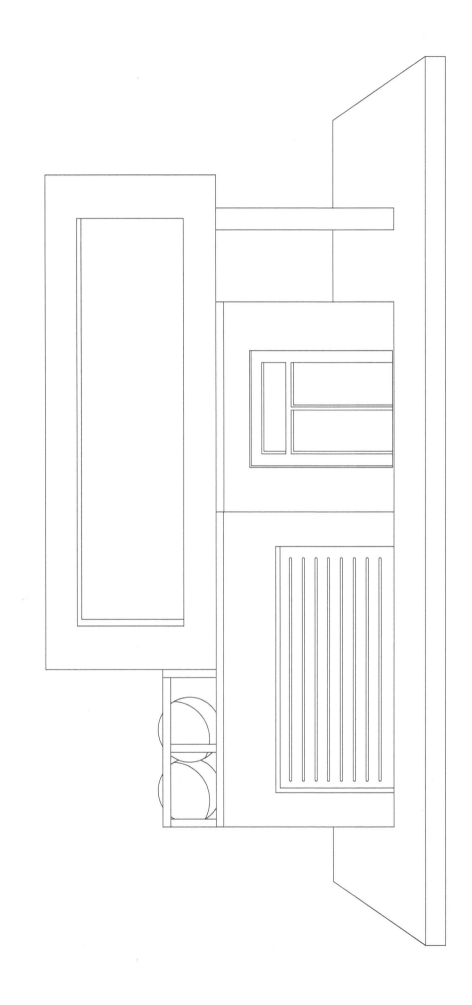

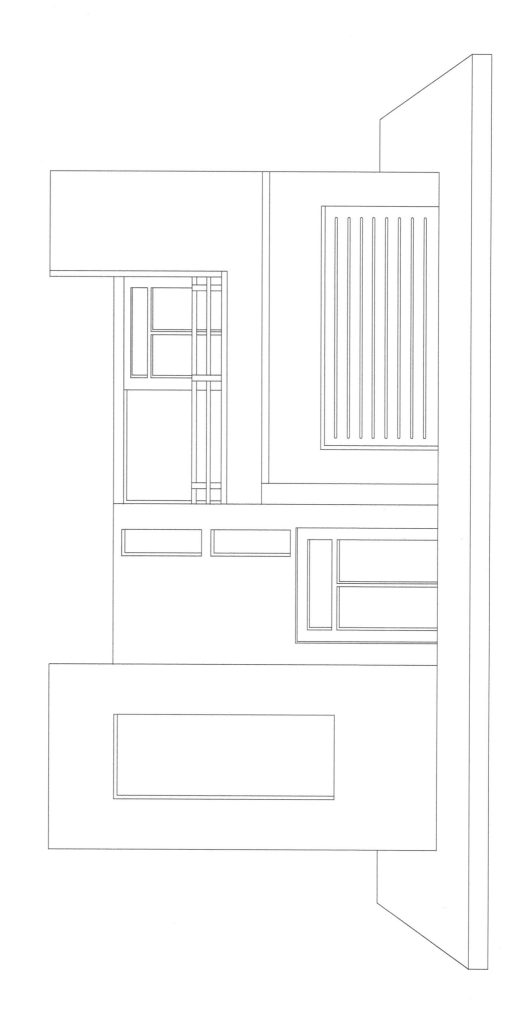

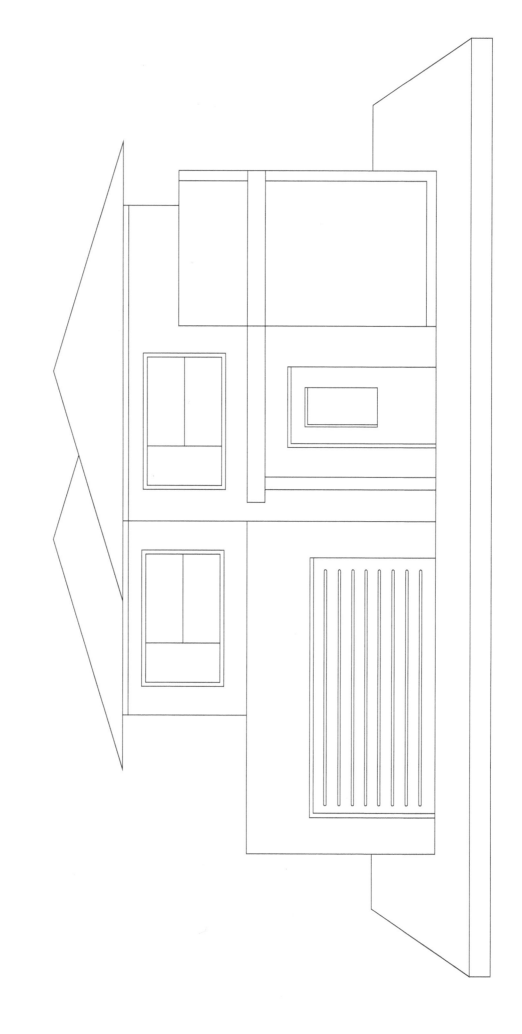

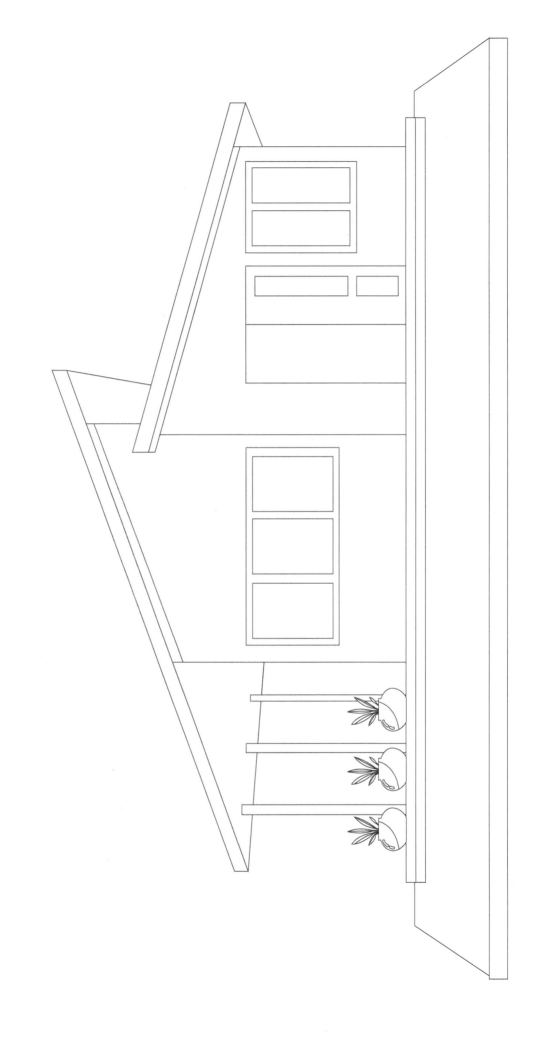

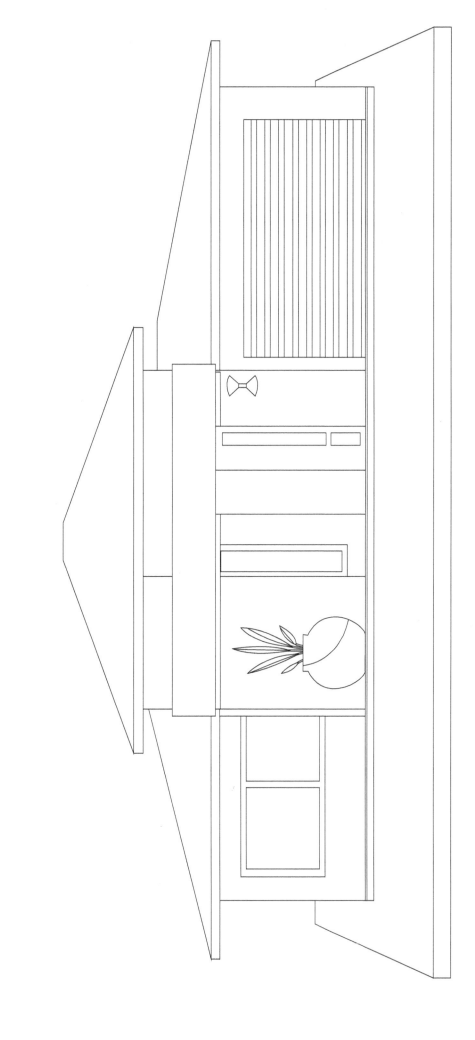

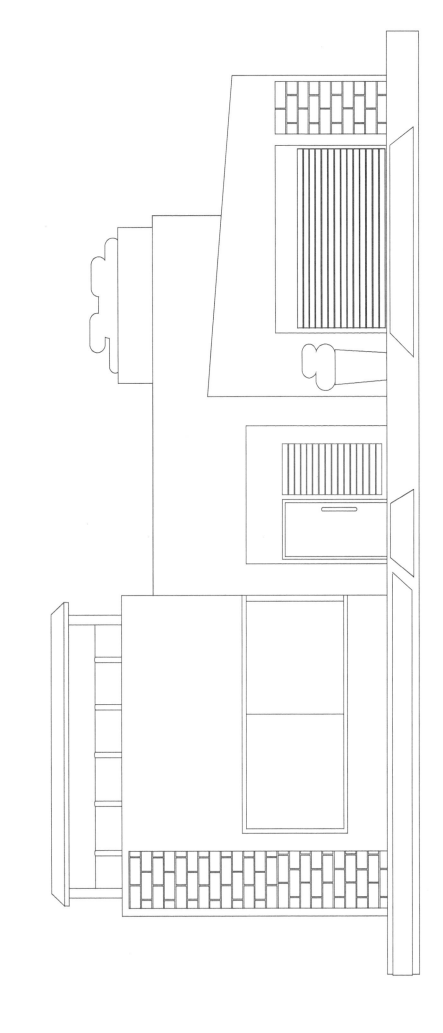

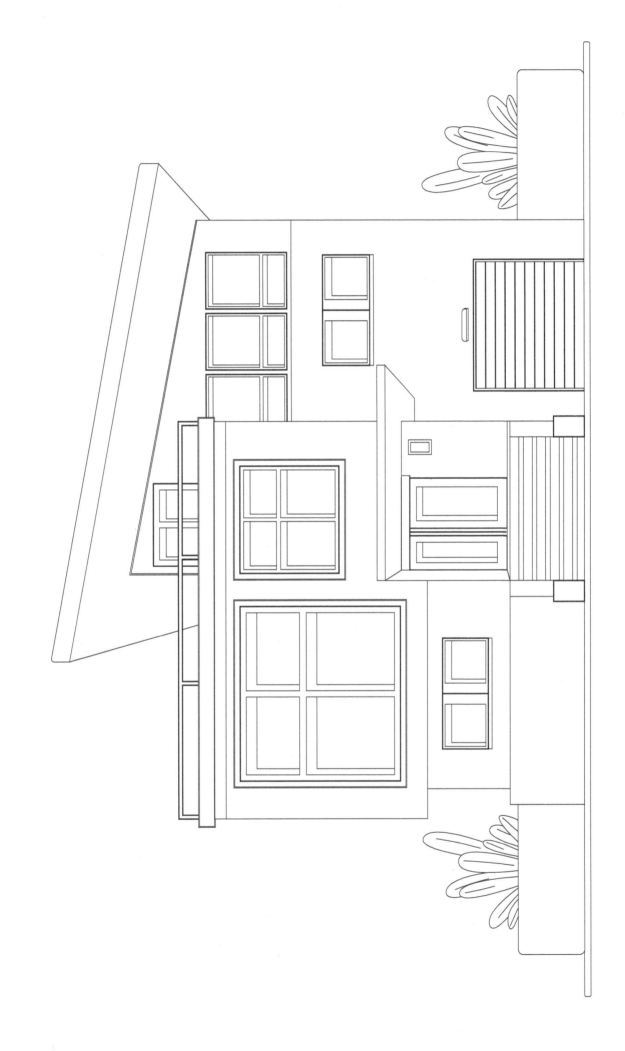

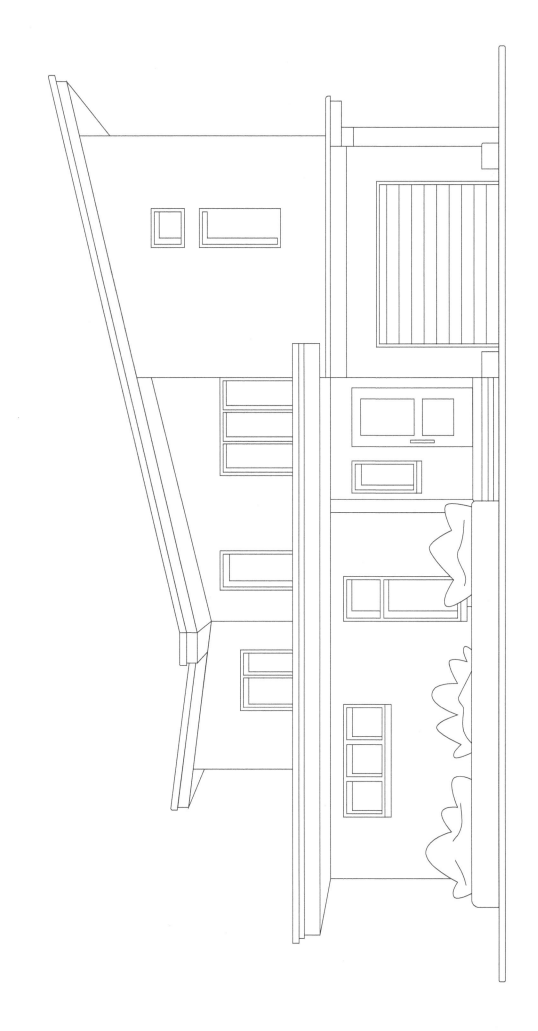

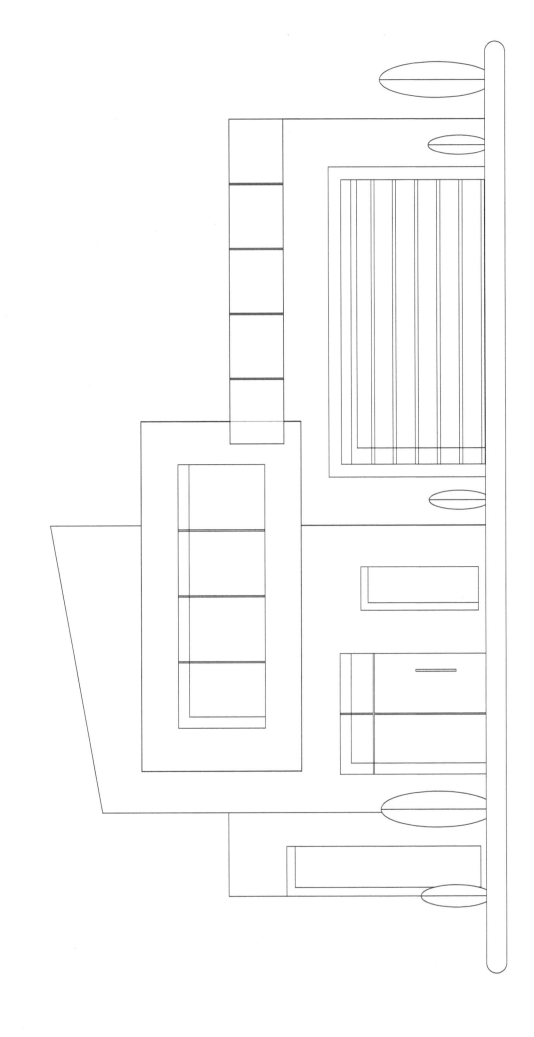

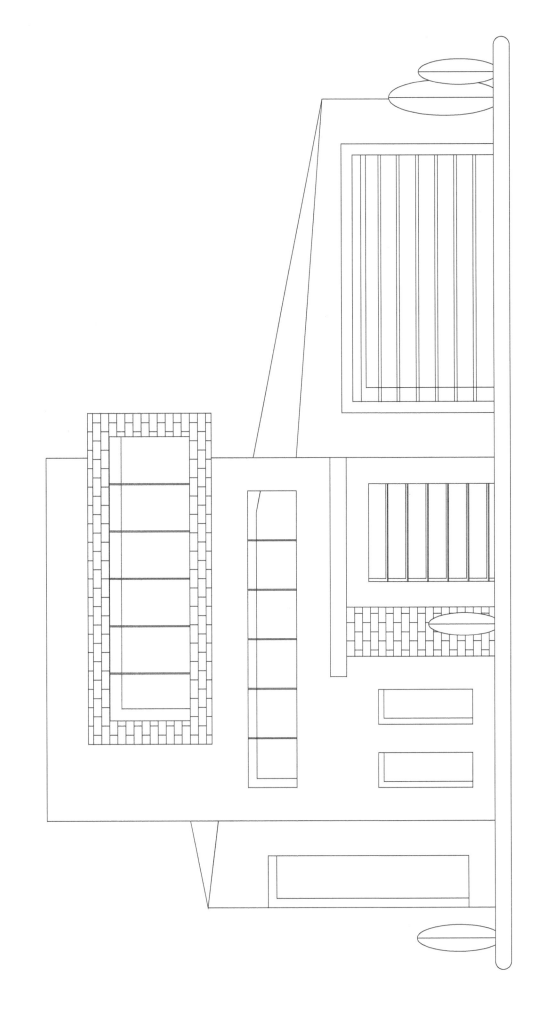

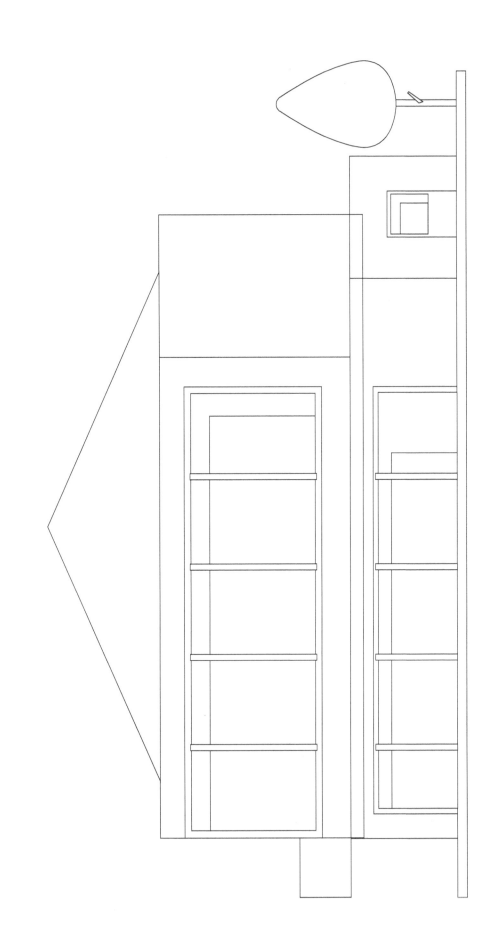

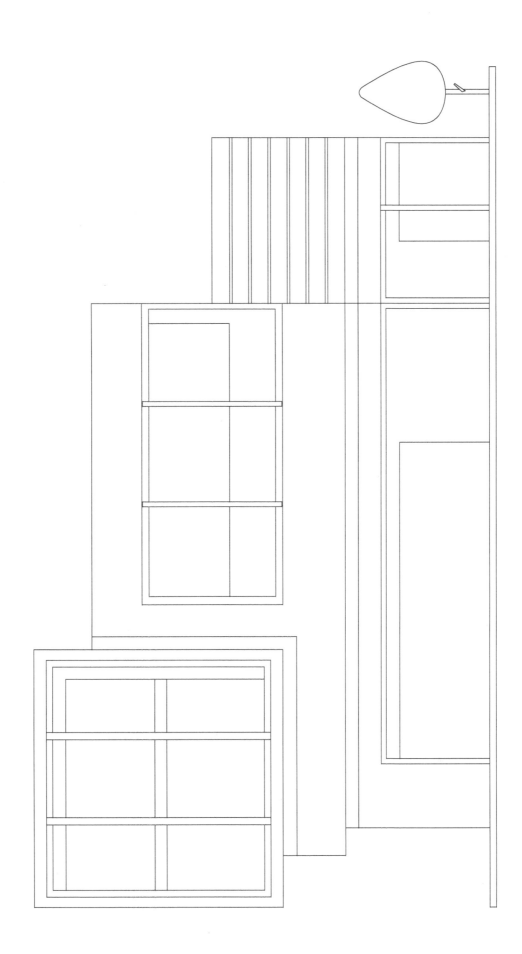

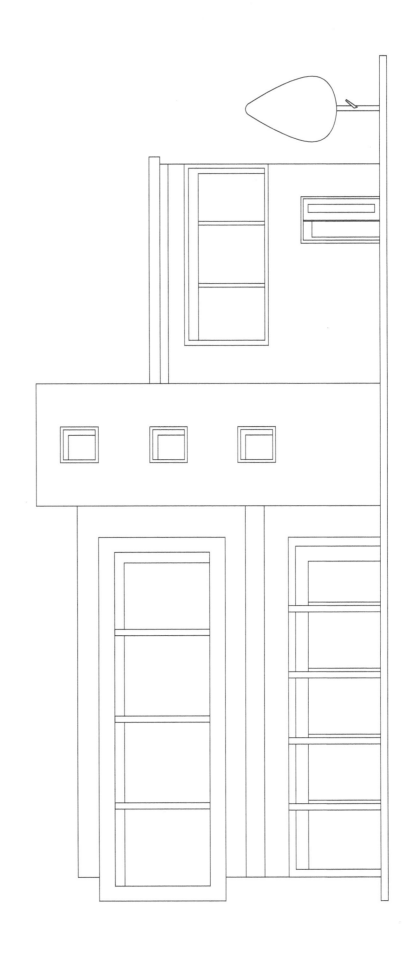

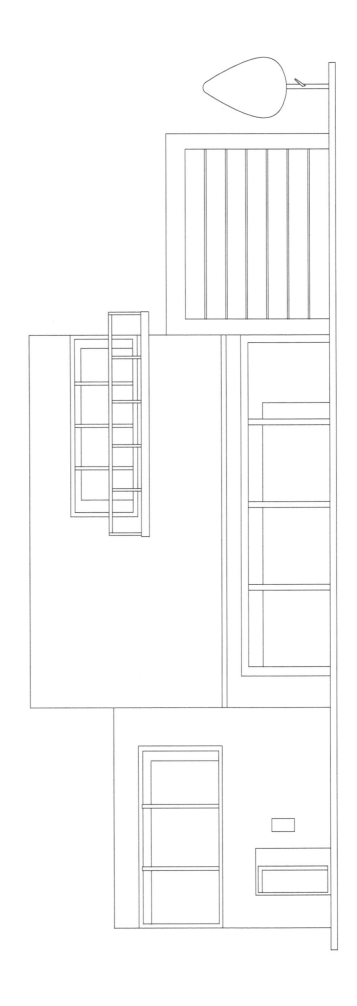

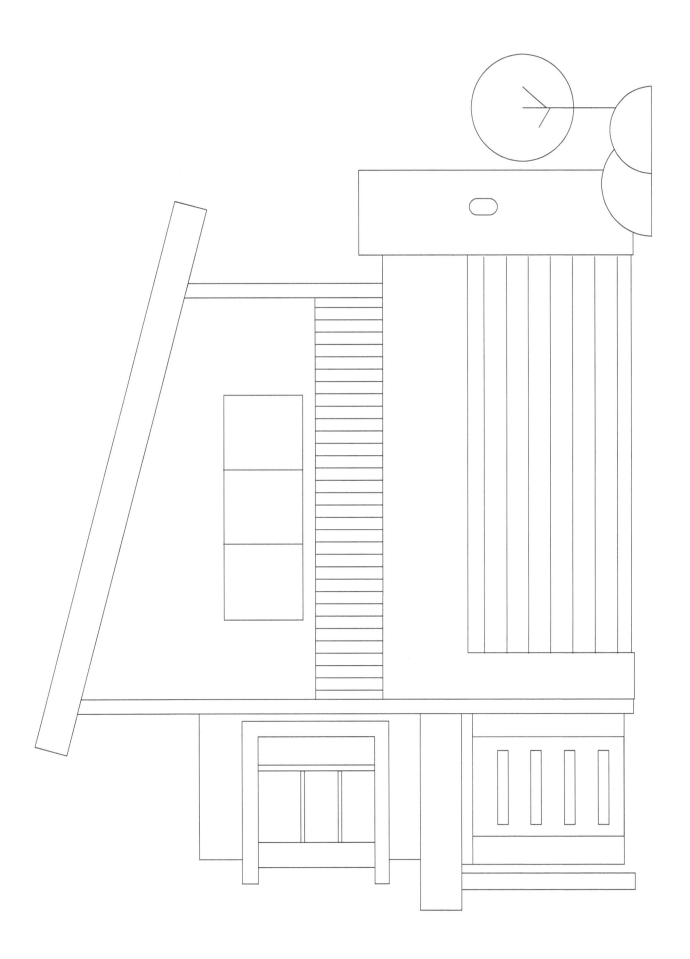

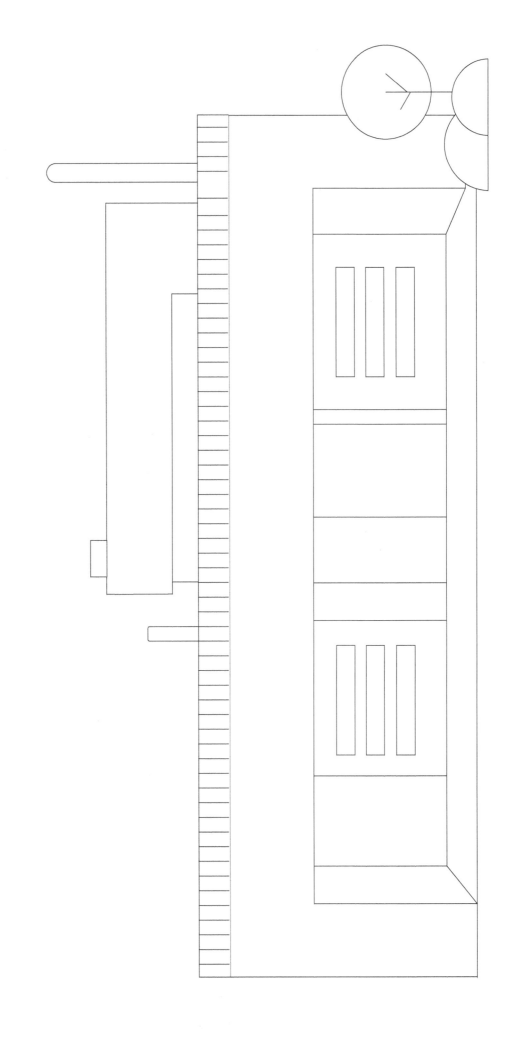

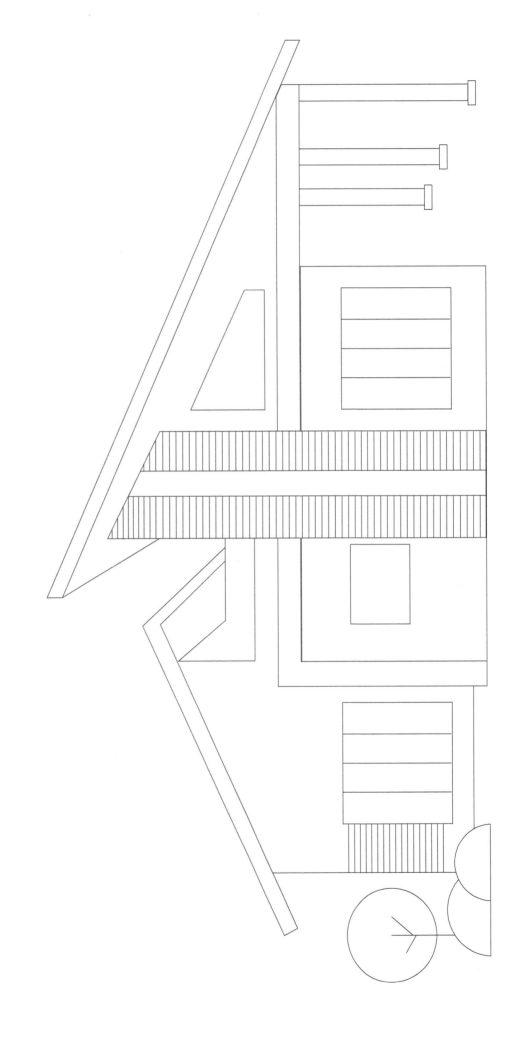

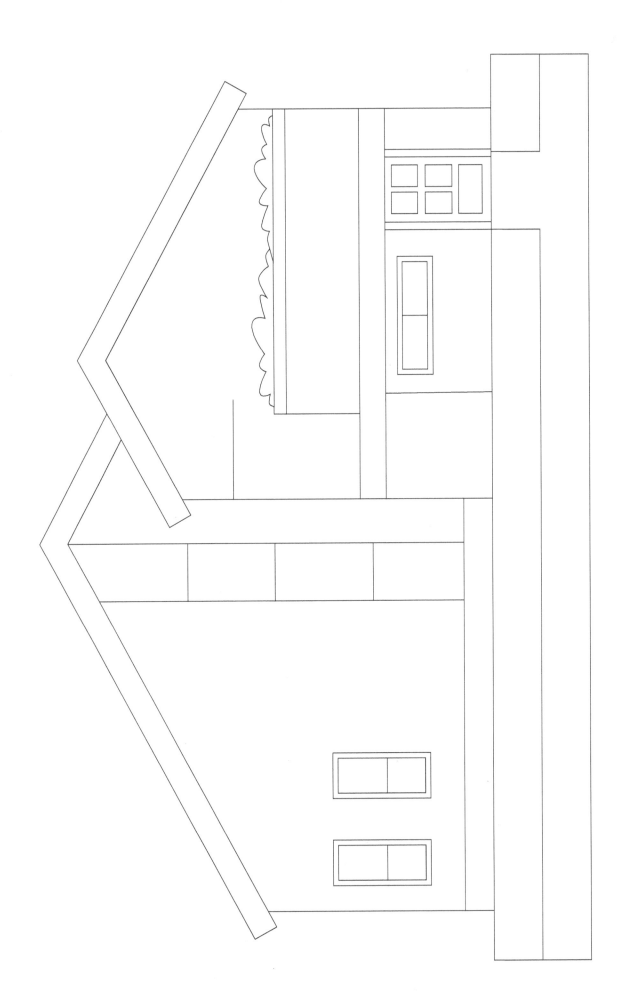

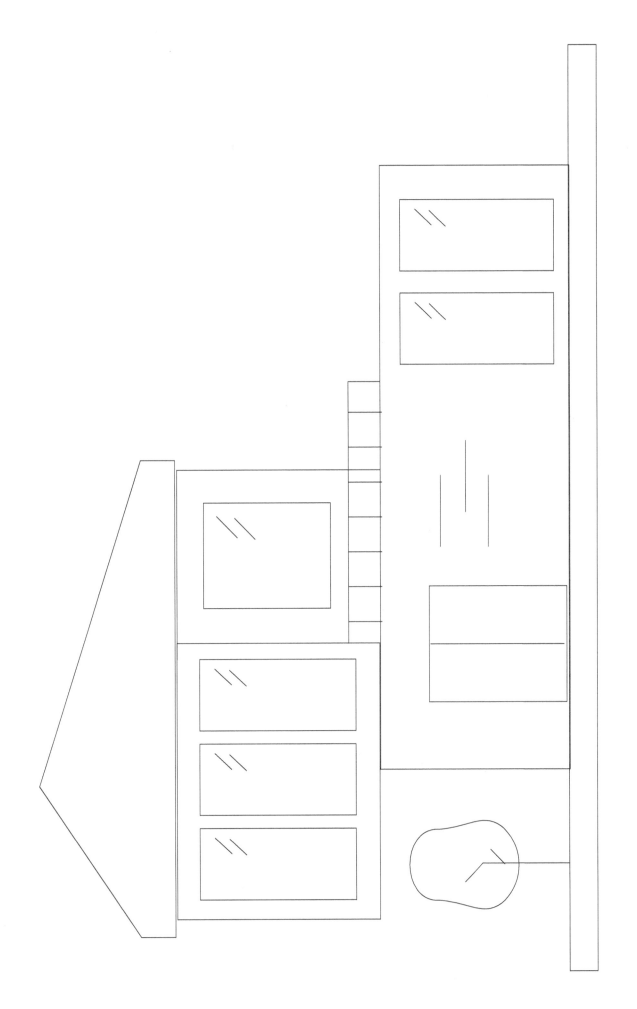

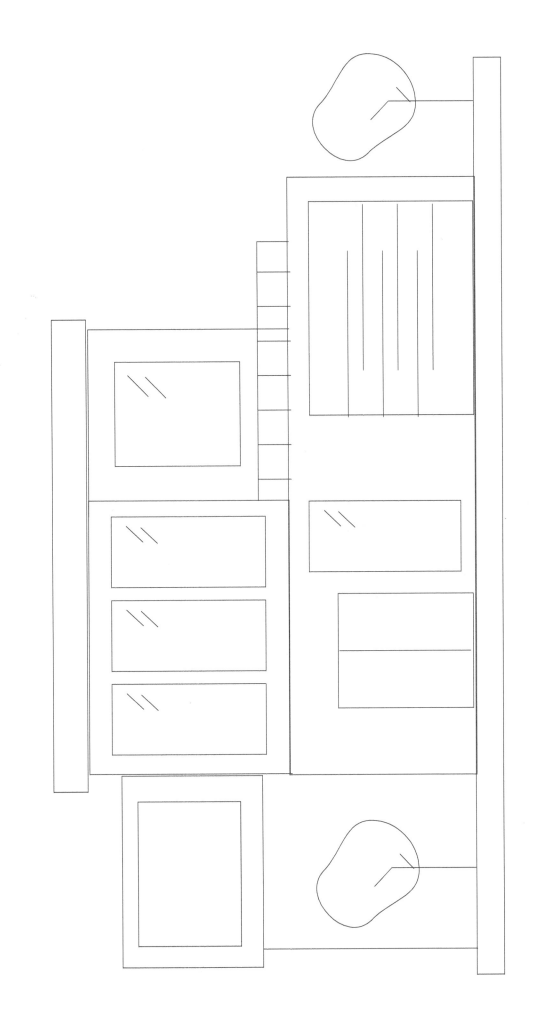

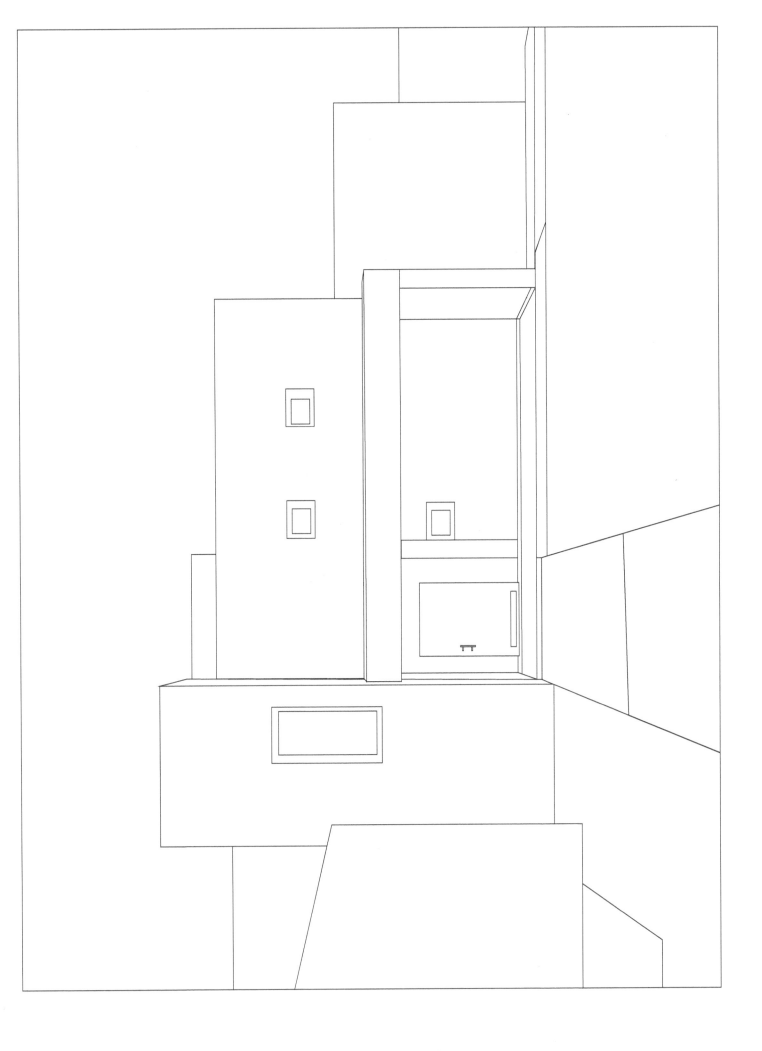

Tips & Tricks
COLORING

Welcome to the MODERN HOUSES Minimalist Art Coloring Book by Paper Dreams Publishing.

Whether you're an architecture enthusiast, a seasoned artist or new to the world of coloring, these 50 minimalist architecture designs are bound to captivate your imagination and soothe your soul.

Are you ready to unleash your inner artist and make the most of your coloring experience? Here are some helpful tips and tricks to enhance your creative journey:

Choose Your Colors Wisely
Start by selecting a color palette that reflects the mood you want to convey. Soft pastels for a calming atmosphere, vibrant hues for a lively touch, or monochromatic tones for an elegant, minimalist look.

Begin with a Test Page
Before diving into your favorite design, try out your chosen colors on a separate page to ensure they harmonize well together and achieve the desired effect.

Layering and Blending
Experiment with layering colors to create depth and dimension. Use lighter shades as a base and darker ones for shading. Blend colors by varying your pressure on the pencil for a smooth transition.

Mindful Coloring
Coloring can be a form of meditation. Focus on each stroke, and let the worries of the day slip away. Enjoy the process as much as the end result.

Tips & Tricks
COLORING

Try Different Techniques

Add variety to your designs by exploring different techniques like stippling, cross--hatching, or even pointillism. These methods can bring your pages to life in unique surprising ways.

Protect Your Work

Since the pages in this book are single-sided, feel free to use markers, gel pens, or even watercolors without worrying about bleed-through. Place a sheet of paper behind the page you're coloring to prevent any transfer of ink to the next design.

Share Your Masterpieces

Your completed pages can easily double as wall art. Frame and hang them to add a touch of elegance to your living space. Your creativity deserves to be showcased!

Find Your Calm

Coloring is not just a creative outlet; it's a powerful stress-relief tool. Take a moment to relax, breathe, and let your worries melt away as you immerse yourself in the world of design.

Enjoy the Journey

Most importantly, savor the process of coloring. It's a journey of self-expression and self-discovery. Let your imagination flow and allow your inner artist to flourish.

We hope these tips and tricks enhance your coloring adventure within the MODERN HOUSES Minimalist Art Coloring Book. May this book not only spark your creativity but also bring you peace and relaxation as you color these modern minimal architecture houses. Happy coloring!

Thank You!

Thank you for your purchase. If you enjoyed this book, please leave us a review!
As a token of our appreciation, we're excited to offer you some fantastic freebies.

VISIT US ONLINE TODAY!
www.paperdreamspublishing.com